Mala Discovers

by Alexandria Pereira

AuthorHouse™
1663 Liberty Drive
Bloomington, IN 47403
www.authorhouse.com
Phone: 833-262-8899

Because of the dynamic nature of the Internet, any web addresses or links contained in this book may have changed since publication and may no longer be valid. The views expressed in this work are solely those of the author and do not necessarily reflect the views of the publisher, and the publisher hereby disclaims any responsibility for them.

This book is printed on acid-free paper.

ISBN: 979-8-8230-0285-1 (sc)
ISBN: 979-8-8230-0286-8 (hc)
ISBN: 979-8-8230-0287-5 (e)

Library of Congress Control Number: 2023904515

Print information available on the last page.

Published by AuthorHouse 04/18/2023

authorHOUSE®

The Mystery of History Series
India
Book 1 or 4

To my grandma, whose life work was dedicated
to children and their pursuit of knowledge.

"Grandma, where do I come from?" asked Mala.

"I am so glad you asked Mala. You know that you are part of a family. Your mother is my child, and my mother is your great-grandmother. And she had a mother too. These are our ancestors, the people that came before you. Mala you are part of a family," said Grandma.

"OK, but where do we come from? It is a mystery to me," asked Mala.

"Well, our family is part of a bigger family. Our neighbors, the people at your school, even the people that work in the stores, are part of our city family. People that live in big cities, like New Delhi, and small cities, like Mandya, are part of our even bigger family.

"We call this even bigger family a country. Our country is called India, and sometimes, we call it Bharat. India is on the continent of Asia. The country of India is shaped like a diamond. Should we go see our country?" asked Grandma.

"Yes, grandma," answered Mala.

"India has many mountains. The Himalayan Mountains are the youngest and tallest mountains on earth. Just like you and I, they are still growing. But they only grow as fast as our fingernails do," said Grandma. "Oh," said Mala.

"India has many rivers. On the Indus River, our early ancestors grew food, to eat and trade. And today the water from the Ganges River helps people and plants grow.

"India also has lakes, like Bhojtal Lake, where you can see cranes, the largest bird in India.

"And there are a lot of forests. Bengal Tigers live in mangrove forests and like to swim. Indian elephants live in scrub, tropical, and deciduous forests and eat with their long trunks," said Grandma.

"Do elephants wash their trucks before they eat?" asked Mala.
"No," laughed Grandma.

"India has the Deccan Plateau. It was formed by lava, from an old volcano. On the plateau, people respect animals and their lives so much, that they let cows walk wherever they want to go. This often causes traffic jams.

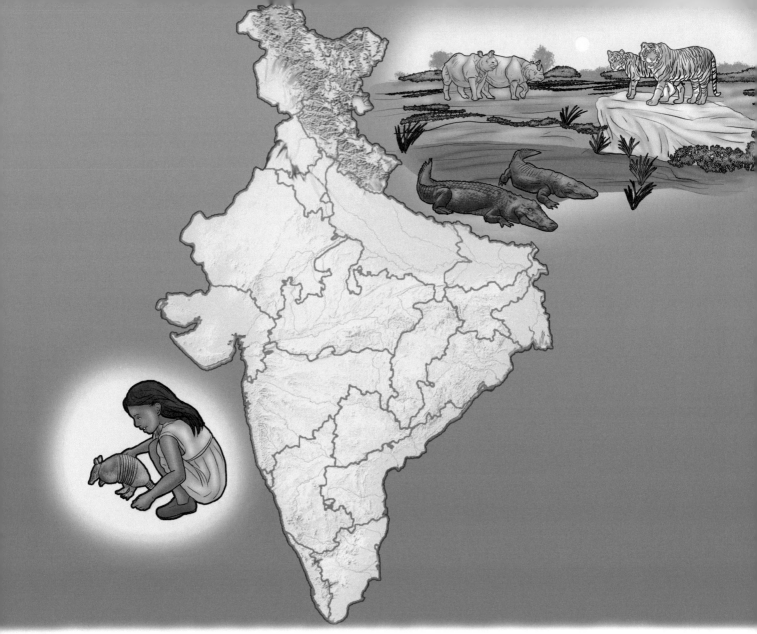

"And India has plains. The plains lie on both sides of the Deccan Plateau. Armadillos live on the coastal plains. Long ago, people thought they were sea monsters," said Grandma.

"Her armor is so hard," said Mala. "On the northern plains, one-horned rhinoceroses still run around, as do tigers and crocodiles.

"There are also deserts, like the Thar Desert, where riding camels is the thing to do.

"India also has beaches, like Goa's beaches, where you can watch sea turtles hatch," said Grandma. "Run little turtles, run to the sea," beckoned Mala.

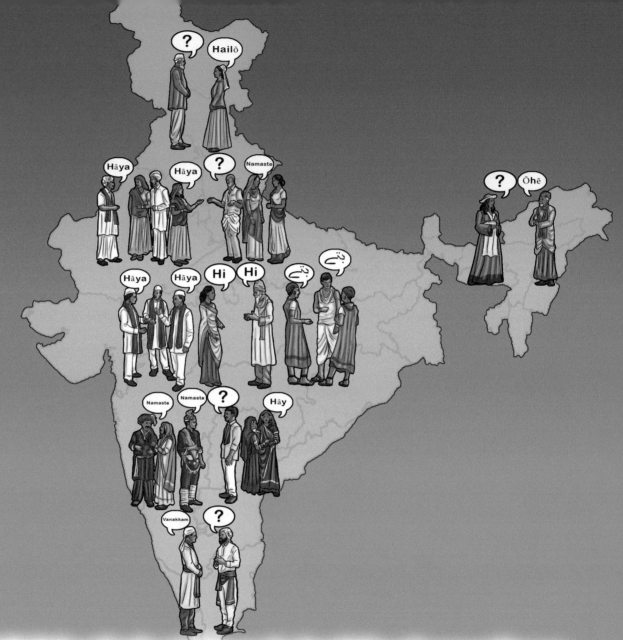

"And India has a lot of people. They speak a lot of different languages. There are twenty-two official languages. This makes it hard for people in different parts of India to understand one another. So now schools teach English, and people use English to talk to someone who does not speak their official language.

"There are also national parks, like the Great Himalayan National Park. Snow leopards live high in the snowy mountains. And mountain goats are not afraid of heights. Griffon vultures fly over our heads, looking for food. Sloth bears look under rocks, for honey, as butterflies dance around," said Grandma. "It tickles," laughed Mala.

"India has beautiful buildings, forts, and temples. The Taj Mahal, Red Fort, and the Golden Temple of Amritsar are all fun to visit.

"India has hills, like the Garo Khasi Jaintia hills. These hills have the highest waterfalls in India, and it is the wettest place on earth," said Grandma.
"I'm glad we brought our raincoats," said Mala.

"And there are six seasons—spring, summer, monsoon, autumn, prewinter, and winter. The seasons work together, to help the people of India grow food, trade, and still have time to play.

In the spring, people enjoy the Festival of Colors, by throwing colored powder on each other and squirting each other with water. Happy Holi, Mala," said Grandma.

"You too Grandma," laughed Mala.

"In summer mornings, people can go for a swim, in the clear ocean waves, and meet a fish.

"During the monsoon season, so much rain falls from the sky that it floods everything. The rain helps people grow a lot of food to eat and trade.

In autumn, you can ride an elephant, to take your crops to market to trade. Mala is your elephant bothering my elephant?" asked Grandma.

"Hehe, yes," laughed Mala.

"In prewinter, people can go on a camel safari in the Thar Desert, just for fun.

In winter, you can play in the snow, in Himachal Pradesh," said Grandma. "Sledding is fun," said Mala.

"India has a lot of farmland, where people grow all kinds of food to eat. And on that farmland, a very long time ago, a dinosaur walked," said Grandma.

"What was it called?" asked Mala.

"The *Rajasaurus narmadensis*, or king lizard. It was smaller but stronger than a T-Rex, and only lived in India. Do you know what other kinds of animals lived in India but do not anymore?" asked Grandma.

"Was it ostrich and giraffe?" replied Mala.
"Yes. They lived in India first, then they all moved to Africa," replied Grandma.

"Here I am, with my grandma. I see how all the mountains, rivers, lakes, forests, plateaus, plains, deserts, beaches, people, national parks, forts, temples, six whole seasons, and farmland are part of my bigger family. I come from this big family, the country of India. My history is no longer a mystery.

Thank you, Grandma," said Mala.
"You are welcome," said Grandma.

Educational Support Activities

Basic Human Needs

We need food to eat, clothing to keep us warm, and shelter to keep us safe and dry.
We need to socialize, to work together.
We need to solve problems, so that we can invent and be creative.

Practical Life and Sensorial Foundation

Plant a seed, water plants, and wash your hands. Why do we do these things?

History

Make a timeline of the Indian seasons. Write, draw, and color it.

Geography and Map Work

Trace a map of India with your finger. Where are the mountains, rivers, plateaus, and beaches?

Science

Explode a controlled volcano, on a big map of India, and watch the Deccan Plateau form.

Earth Science

Push two pieces of heavier paper together, to form the Himalayan Mountains—plate tectonics.

Peace Curriculum

Work together, to solve a simple problem, and be proud of your accomplishment.

Printed in the United States
by Baker & Taylor Publisher Services